Ways to Paint Your Face

Written by Lucy Monroe
Illustrated by Larry Nolte

Cover photograph by Sia Aryai

Lowell 🏠 House
Juvenile
Los Angeles

Contemporary Books
Chicago

⭐ IMPORTANT! ⭐

BEFORE USING THIS BOOK: Ask a parent or a responsible adult for permission to use paints on your face. Also, it is important to remember that people react differently to substances used on the skin, especially on the face. Before applying ANY paint to your skin, test for an allergic reaction by first dabbing a little paint on your arm, waiting at least four hours, then washing it off and looking for any signs of irritation. If you do have an allergic reaction of any kind, do not use any paint on your face. If you don't, open this book and let's get started!

Library of Congress Catalog Card Number: 92-549

ISBN: 1-56565-029-8

10 9 8 7 6 5 4 3 2 1

Getting Started with Face Painting

Face painting began thousands of years ago and has flourished throughout many different cultures as part of ritual, celebration, and performance. Today face painting remains a living art, drawing kids of all ages into the mystery and fun of creating their very own monsters, animals, and magical creatures.

50 Nifty Ways to Paint Your Face encourages you to explore your face-painting talents. It's easy—just follow our step-by-step instructions and refer to our lively illustrations! And for extra fun, we've included some Nifty Facts about the faces you'll be trying on.

But before you get started, you must check with a parent to see if it's okay for you to use paints on your face. If the answer is yes, then read the section below. It's a step-by-step "how to" for face painting, and it even includes a recipe for making your own face paint.

Materials and Instructions

Follow these easy instructions and guidelines for using various materials and you'll be well on your way to creating fabulous faces.

1. To start, you'll need paint, of course! Use water-soluble crayons or water-based, nontoxic cosmetic paints that will come off easily with soap and water. You can buy face-painting materials at cosmetic and beauty supply stores, costume shops, hobby shops, and anywhere arts and crafts supplies are sold. Some safe brands include such water-based paints as Funny Face and Kryolan Aqua Colors, or Joe Blasco liner colors, which

3

are made from wax. For those of you who'd prefer to make your own paints, there's an easy recipe included at the end of this section!

2. Although any of the paints suggested here will come off easily with soap and water, an even more effective way of removing paint from your face is to use your mom's makeup remover, cleansing cream, or cold cream. Petroleum jelly will work, too, but do *not* use baby oil, as it will sting your eyes. If you do use soap and water, remember soap will sting your eyes, too.

3. Three sizes of brushes—small, medium, and large—can be used to paint your face. Any brand of brush will work, including a makeup brush. You can buy brushes at any of the stores mentioned earlier as well as at hardware stores. Cotton swabs make good "extra" brushes, too. And, of course, you can use your fingers!

4. You will need two small cups of water to clean your brushes. It's a good idea to follow the cleaning instructions on the face painting materials you buy, but for most brands of face paints, including the homemade recipe, you'll need to dip your brush in water before using each paint. The brush should be wet, but not dripping. The second cup of water is for cleaning your brush before using a different paint.

5. Makeup makes a great tool for face painting! You can use lipstick, eyeliner pencil, and eye shadow in all colors. Black eyeliner pencil is especially useful when outlining shapes on your face. It is important to buy new makeup, since old makeup may contain harmful bacteria.

6. A clean sponge (cut into small pieces) works well for covering large areas with paint.

7. Cotton balls can be used to decorate many of the faces, and petroleum jelly makes a great "paste" with which to secure the cotton to your face.

8. Charcoal comes in handy for several of our faces. Some safe brands recommended by art-supply stores are Kole and Vine. Quick strokes and touch-ups work best with this nifty tool. Regular charcoal pencils and barbecue charcoal can also be used, *but only if they are free of chemicals.*

9. Don't forget the glitter for those special faces! Glitter can be sprinkled over petroleum jelly that has been dabbed onto your face, or applied over paint before the paint is fully dry. Be careful not to get any in your eyes!

10. Paper towels, rags, tissues, and even your dad's old shirt (worn as a smock) will help keep you clean as you apply your face paint. Be sure not to wear a T-shirt or other article of clothing that has to be taken off over the head. You might smear your creation!

Face Paint Recipe

PARENTAL SUPERVISION REQUIRED

Here's an easy way to make your own face paints. Just ask a parent to add the items listed below to a grocery list. Then follow our easy recipe and you'll have nontoxic paints that will help you make wonderful faces and will wash off easily with soap and water.

What You'll Need:

- 1 tablespoon unflavored gelatin
- cold water
- ½ cup cornstarch
- 4 tablespoons dishwashing liquid
- food coloring (as many colors as you like)
- 1 empty plastic ice tray

1. Pour the gelatin into a mixing bowl and add ⅓ cup cold water. Stir the mixture until it is dissolved, then set it aside.
2. Next, pour 2 ½ cups of water into a saucepan and add the cornstarch. While stirring, heat the mixture until it boils. Then, reduce the heat so the mixture simmers. Continue stirring until the cornstarch is totally dissolved and fully thickened.
3. Now turn off the heat and blend in the gelatin mixture from step 1.
4. Stir in the dishwashing liquid.
5. Once the mixture has cooled down, spoon it evenly into each of the different compartments of your ice tray. Then start adding drops of food coloring to each compartment, one color per compartment. The more drops you add, the richer your colors will look. You can also try mixing colors. See what color you get when you mix red with blue. Here's a hint—grape juice is the same color!
6. After your paint is completely cool, you can apply it to your face with your fingers or a paintbrush.

Homework Helper

Turn your face into a clean blackboard, then nab some volunteers to do some math on it. The "chalk" *they* use won't squeak across your face!

What You'll Need

- black, white, and brown (mix of green and red) paints
- paintbrush
- sponge

Directions

1. First, create a square blackboard by mixing black and white paints to make dark gray. Then use the sponge to put the mixture onto your face. Make sure to leave enough room for the frame you will paint in the next step.

2. Now draw in the blackboard's thick rectangular frame with brown paint.

3. After your blackboard is dry, have a friend use white paint as "chalk" to paint a short math problem on the board. Then have another friend paint on the answer!

NOTE: For each of the 50 nifty face painting ideas in this book, you'll see a number in the upper right-hand corner. This indicates the level of difficulty of each face painting idea, 1 paintbrush being the easiest, 3 paintbrushes being the hardest.

Dr. Jekyll and Mr. Hyde

And you think *you're* moody? With a little paint, you can turn your face into a split personality!

What You'll Need

- green and gray (mix of black and white) paints
- paintbrush
- black eyeliner pencil
- charcoal (see Instruction 8 on page 4)
- red paint or lipstick

Directions

1. First, using the charcoal, draw a jagged line running down the middle of your face.

2. For the monster side (Mr. Hyde), mix green and gray paint to create a "hideous" skin tone. Black charcoal can be used under the eyes for that "sunken in" look.

3. Don't forget to pencil in scars, stitches, and a bushy eyebrow with the black eyeliner as shown. Bloody sores wouldn't "hurt" either. They can be achieved by using dabs of red paint or lipstick.

4. The normal side of your face (Dr. Jekyll) doesn't need any more than your own sweet face!

Creepy Crawlers

Now it's time to get really gross and paint the insects that have always bugged you! Make this face and invite your creepiest friends to a party!

What You'll Need

- any paints you choose
- paintbrush
- black eyeliner pencil

Directions

1. With black eyeliner, draw the outlines of a worm, an ant, a beetle, or any bug of your choice on your cheeks. See the illustrations for ideas.

2. Now color in your insect "passengers" with different combinations of paints. How about gory green beetles or bright orange worms? The more disgusting the bugs, the better!

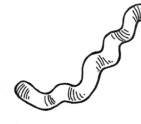

One Step Further

What You'll Need:
a flyswatter

Does all this buzzing bother you? Why not carry a real flyswatter around with you when you wear this face and let the bugs beware!

Sweety Tweety

This face is definitely for the birds!

What You'll Need

- yellow, brown, green, red, and white paints
- black eyeliner pencil
- paintbrush
- petroleum jelly
- cotton balls

Directions

1. With brown paint, draw a branch running from one cheek to the other cheek. Then clean your paintbrush and add leaves to your branch with green paint.

2. Next, look carefully at the illustration to help you draw the bird. Outline your feathered friend with black eyeliner pencil. Make sure your bird is perched proudly on the branch.

3. Now carefully color in the bird. Use red paint to make a robin or yellow paint to make a canary.

4. On the other cheek, paint a cozy nest resting on the branch. Use brown paint and black eyeliner pencil to highlight your nest's tiny twigs.

5. Finally, wad some cotton balls up like cookie dough, using water to shape the cotton into eggs. Then put your "eggs" in the nest, using petroleum jelly to secure them.

Nifty Fact

Birds are the only animals with feathers!

Monkey Shines

Your friends and family are sure to go ape over this face. So paint it on, grab a banana, and swing through your neighborhood!

What You'll Need

- brown and black paints
- sponge
- paintbrush

Directions

1. First, sponge brown paint all over your face and let it dry.

2. Next, mix some brown and black paints to make dark brown. Then sponge this darker color around your mouth and chin. Also, paint a dark brown "V" on your forehead to add to your monkey's darkened features.

3. Now paint black rings around each nostril to create a monkey nose. Then paint two more black rings around each eye to create that deep-set look.

One Step Further

What You'll Need:
yellow construction paper • scissors

If you can't get a banana from the kitchen, draw and cut out a banana using yellow construction paper. Then carry it around with you as you romp around your "jungle" neighborhood.

Highway Head

Get yourself in gear with this one. Grab some paint and hit the road!

What You'll Need

- green, blue, red, yellow, black, and white paints
- paintbrush
- black eyeliner pencil
- sponge

Directions

1. First, with the eyeliner pencil, draw in the outline of your highway. Make two vertical lines as wide apart as you can from your forehead to your chin. If you want, you can let your highway narrow by drawing it down your neck, too. Then, with a sponge and some black paint, lay down some asphalt between the lines you just drew, as shown.

2. Once your blacktop has dried, paint in a dotted yellow line. Your highway should be divided right down the middle of your face, from your forehead to your chin.

3. Next, draw a green rectangle on your right cheek and a blue rectangle on your left cheek. These will be your cars, viewed as if you were looking at them from an airplane!

4. Now, because you're driving at nighttime, you'd better turn on your lights. To do this, paint two tiny white dots (headlights) on the top (front) of your blue car. Do the same on your green car, but because it is going the other way, paint the dots on the other end of the car. Then draw little white streams of light coming from each headlight, using the illustration to guide you.

5. Finally, your cars need taillights, too. Add them in with two tiny red lights on the back end of each of your cars. Then buckle up and drive safely!

Nifty Fact Did you know that, contrary to popular belief, Henry Ford did not invent the automobile? Charles and Frank Duryea built the first successful gasoline-powered car in the United States in 1895. And the steam-powered car was invented more than a century before that—in 1769 by Nicholas-Joseph Cugnot of France.

Madame Butterfly

You can test your wings with this face! Your beautiful butterfly will have hearts fluttering as you fly by.

What You'll Need

- any three paint colors you choose
- paintbrush
- black eyeliner pencil
- petroleum jelly
- glitter

Directions

1. Using black eyeliner pencil, draw a circle just above the center of your eyebrows for the butterfly's head. Then, for its body, draw a thick, solid-black line down your nose. The body should begin just below the butterfly's head and end just below your nose.

2. Now it's time to come out of your cocoon! Draw the upper part of the wings above your eyes and the lower part of the wings on your cheeks as shown. Once again, your painting tool is the black eyeliner pencil.

3. Fill in your wings with any color of paint you choose. If you like, create a design using several colors!

4. Dab petroleum jelly on the parts of the wings where you want to put glitter, then sprinkle away. Now you're gorgeous, so spread your wings and you're on your way!

5. Finally, add black antennae on your forehead. Or, go one step further and read on!

One Step Further

What You'll Need:
headband • pipe cleaners

For more realistic antennae, secure two pipe cleaners to a plastic head-band by twisting the ends around it. Roll the other ends into little knobs as shown. Now your antennae are ready to receive good vibes!

Nifty Fact

Did you know that there are 15,000 to 20,000 different kinds of butterflies around the world? They can be as tiny as pygmy blue butterflies from western North America, which have a half-inch wingspan, or as large as bird wing butterflies from Indonesia, which have a ten-inch wingspan.

Cheshire Cat

Alice had to go down a rabbit hole to find a cat like this but you can create one in just a few easy steps.

What You'll Need

- brown, white, and black paints
- paintbrush
- black eyeliner pencil
- sponge

Directions

1. First, turn some brown paint into a tan color by mixing in a few drops of white paint. Then, with your sponge, dab this new paint all over your face for a "furry cat" look.

2. Once your fur is dry, outline a wide grin with a black eyeliner pencil, extending your lips to your ears as shown.

3. Now, with black eyeliner again, draw in a few extra teeth to fill in your new big mouth.

4. Paint in your new dental work with white paint for a pearly-white look.

5. Black whiskers are next to make you even more catlike. And don't forget to give yourself a solid-black nose.

6. Finally, think of your favorite kitty and mimic its markings using the paintbrush and the brown paint, white paint, and the tan color you created in step 1. When you're finished, you'll definitely have something to grin about!

One Step Further

What You'll Need:
construction paper • scissors • cotton • stapler • glue

Create kitty ears by first making a headband to attach them to. Begin by cutting a strip of construction paper into a band that fits around your head (the paper should match the colors of your Cheshire Cat face). Then staple the ends together. Next, cut out two triangular ears from the same piece of construction paper and staple them to the front of your new paper headband. Finally, glue tiny pieces of cotton to the inside of each ear, and don't be surprised if someone tries to scratch behind them!

Pinocchio

We'd be lying if we said this wasn't a funny face. But only your nose really knows!

What You'll Need

- black and red paints
- paintbrush

Directions

1. Start Pinocchio by painting black lines from the sides of your mouth to your chin.

2. Next, again with black paint, draw big "doll" eyes and eyelashes using the illustration for tips.

3. Finally, how about using red paint to give your puppet rosy cheeks? Soon you'll see why Pinocchio's father, Geppetto, loved him!

One Step Further

What You'll Need:
putty • cap with feather •
2 pieces of construction paper • stapler • scissors • tape

Do you remember that Pinocchio's nose grew when he lied? To make your own nose "grow," mold some putty, as shown, and press it to the sides of your nose until it sticks. Then, how about going even further by wearing a cap with a feather in it? If you don't have a feathered cap, you can create one by taking a square piece of construction paper (approximately 1 foot by 1 foot, depending on the size of your head), folding it into a cone, and stapling it. Then cut out a feather from another piece of paper and tape it to the top of your hat. Now you look more like Pinocchio than ever!

Jack-O'-Lantern

Whether you wear this fun face for Halloween or any other time of the year, you'll only need a paintbrush to carve this pumpkin!

What You'll Need

- orange, green, and black paints
- paintbrush
- black eyeliner pencil
- sponge

Directions

1. To begin turning yourself into a jack-o'-lantern, use black eyeliner to draw the outline of a pumpkin on your face. Your own eyes, nose, and mouth will be the same as the pumpkin's.

2. Then sponge orange paint inside your pumpkin's outline.

3. Now paint a green stem on your forehead. (Your pumpkin had to grow from somewhere, didn't it?)

4. Next, use eyeliner to make black triangles around your eyes and nose. Fill in the triangles with black paint.

5. Finally, blacken out your two front teeth with eyeliner pencil for real "trick or treat" spirit. Then just put a twinkle in your eye and you'll light up your jack-o'-lantern brighter than any candle could!

Nifty Fact

Before Americans used carved pumpkins for their Halloween jack-o'-lanterns, people in England and Ireland carved out potatoes, beets, and turnips to use as lanterns.

Romping Rabbit

Hop to it and paint this bouncing bunny face that's perfect for Easter, springtime, or any day of the year.

What You'll Need

- white, black, and pink paints
- paintbrush (fine)

Directions

1. First, paint a large white circle on each cheek to show your rabbit's high cheekbones.

2. Then, using black paint and a fine paintbrush, draw two large rabbit teeth starting on your bottom lip and continuing down toward your chin. Fill in the teeth with white paint.

3. Now draw on wiggly whiskers and tiny freckles with black eyeliner pencil, as well as a pink bunny nose on the tip of your own!

One Step Further

What You'll Need:
white and pink construction paper • scissors • stapler

Give your rabbit floppy ears by cutting them from white construction paper and stapling them to the front of a headband (for how to make a headband, see Cheshire Cat, p. 16). If you want, line the inside of each ear with pink construction paper. Then grab a carrot and munch away!

Yummy Cone Head

With a face this delicious, you'll be hard to resist, especially on a hot day!

What You'll Need

- brown, white, and pink paints
- paintbrush
- black eyeliner pencil
- multicolored glitter

Directions

1. Using black eyeliner, draw a waffle cone on the bottom part of your face. The narrow part of the cone should be on your chin; the top of the cone should cross the middle of your nose.

2. Now paint the inside of the cone with tan-colored paint (for how to make this color, see Cheshire Cat, page 15). If you like, you can add texture to your cone by painting in crisscrossed lines using the black eyeliner.

3. Here comes the yummy part! Choose your favorite flavor—pink for cherry, yellow for banana, brown for chocolate, any "tasty" color you like. Then paint a scoop of ice cream on top of the cone. If you want, you could even paint a drip or two melting down your cone.

4. Before the paint is completely dry, top your ice cream with multicolored glitter for sprinkles. You'll look so tasty you might want to start licking your own face—but remember, paint won't taste like ice cream!

Tic-Tac-Toe

You'll never be "board" with this playful face. Ask your friends and family to join you for a game!

What You'll Need

- black, blue, and red paints
- paintbrush
- petroleum jelly
- cotton balls

Directions

1. Begin by painting a tic-tac-toe board with black paint on your face. Draw two vertical lines and two horizontal lines that crisscross each other. When you're finished, your nose should be in the middle box as shown.

2. Now dab spots of petroleum jelly inside each box. This will be your "glue" for sticking on the game pieces you will make in the next step.

3. Take five cotton balls and paint red dots on them. On five more, paint blue dots. These will be your game markers.

4. Now it's time to play tic-tac-toe. First, find a friend to play with. Then look in the mirror so you can play, too. Give your friend the red dots and you take the blue dots (or vice versa). Each of you will now take turns sticking markers on your game board face. You know the rules of the game!

A Horse of a Different Color

Quit horsing around and paint a horse that's black and white all over. What kind of horse is that? A zebra, of course!

What You'll Need

- white and black paints
- paintbrush
- sponge
- talcum powder

Directions

1. Begin by dipping your sponge in white paint and turning your entire face white as a ghost.

2. After your face dries, draw vertical black stripes all over your face as shown. If you like, paint the stripes all the way down your neck, too. Paint as many stripes as you can and your horse of a different color will almost be ready to ride.

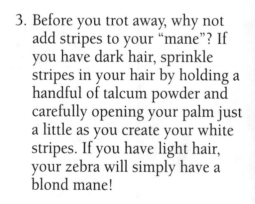

3. Before you trot away, why not add stripes to your "mane"? If you have dark hair, sprinkle stripes in your hair by holding a handful of talcum powder and carefully opening your palm just a little as you create your white stripes. If you have light hair, your zebra will simply have a blond mane!

A Real Patriot

Let's hear it for the red, white, and blue! You'll have friends saying the "Pledge of Allegiance" and singing "Yankee Doodle Dandy" when they see this face march by.

What You'll Need

- red, white, blue, and brown paints
- paintbrush
- black eyeliner pencil

Directions

1. First, draw a square across your face with the eyeliner pencil. This will be the outline of your flag. Then draw another square over your right eye.

2. Now, with white paint, make a solid white star in the middle of your square and let it dry. Although a real flag has 50 five-pointed stars (one for each of the 50 states), you will be able to paint only one.

3. Once your star has dried, carefully fill in the rest of the square with blue paint.

4. Next, paint as many as 13 stripes—seven red and six white—across your face. These stand for the original 13 colonies. You may be able to paint only five or six stripes altogether, but if you can, paint up to 13!

23

5. Finally, how about "hanging" your flag on a flagpole? You can use brown paint for a real-wood look and your neck as the base. Then pick up a little flag if you have one, and wave it like a real patriot!

Nifty Fact

Did you know that when our forefathers were designing the flag they chose red, white, and blue because of the values they symbolized? Red stands for courage, white for purity, and blue for justice.

Frog Witch

Which is it, a frog or a witch? No matter which it is, your friends and family will love this face—warts and all!

What You'll Need

- green, black, and white paints
- paintbrush
- petroleum jelly
- cotton balls
- sponge

Directions

1. Begin making your frog-witch face by preparing your warts. Roll tiny pieces of cotton into balls and paint them green. They'll need to be completely dry before sticking them on your face.

2. Now it's time to make your froggy face. What color are frogs? Green, of course! Sponge green paint from ear to ear and from forehead to chin. If you want, a green neck would be froggy, too.

3. Next, with black paint, draw a half circle over each eye past your eyebrows. Then fill in the half circles with white paint for freaky frog-witch eyes.

4. Following the illustration, use black and green paints mixed together to paint on a nose and creepy eyeballs.

5. Now stick your warts (cotton balls) on your face using petroleum jelly to keep them secure.

25

Eensy-Weensy Spider

You'll get all tangled up when you make this face. But don't get too caught up and run up a waterspout!

What You'll Need

- black paint
- paintbrush (very fine)

Directions

1. Using black paint and a very fine paintbrush, draw the beginning of a spiderweb on one cheek.

2. Next, finish off your spiderweb as shown.

3. Now, with black paint, draw a spider in your web. An example of a spider has been provided. If you like, make the spider a creepy color or give it a speckled texture.

Nifty Fact

More than 30,000 different kinds of *known* spider species creep and crawl about the earth. Scientists estimate there may be as many as 20,000 to 70,000 more kinds of spiders waiting to be discovered!

Tennis, Anyone?

String your face with paint, throw in a ball, and head for the courts!

What You'll Need

- black and white paints
- paintbrush
- black eyeliner pencil
- petroleum jelly
- yellow construction paper
- scissors

Directions

1. Begin your racket by painting in its black frame. Make sure that the "face" of the racket takes up most of your own face. The handle of the racket should continue down your neck as shown.

2. Now draw in the strings of the racket using the eyeliner pencil so the lines are very thin.

3. You can't play tennis without a ball, so cut a circle out of your construction paper, draw tennis ball lines on it with white paint, and stick it on your racket face with petroleum jelly. Now get ready to "serve" your friends a really fun face!

Nifty Fact

A sportswoman named Mary Ewing Outerbridge introduced tennis to the United States in 1874. Because of the popularity and skill of such tennis greats as Chris Evert, Martina Navratilova, Arthur Ashe, John McEnroe, Boris Becker, Steffi Graf, Ivan Lendl, Michael Chang, and Monica Seles, it is one of America's favorite sports.

Batter Up!

It's as American as apple pie! Step up to the plate with this face and you'll hit a home run!

What You'll Need

- green, brown, and white paints
- paintbrush
- black eyeliner pencil
- sponge

Directions

1. Start your baseball face by making a playing field. Take a sponge and rub brown paint on your face in the shape of a baseball diamond.

2. Next, using white paint and the paintbrush, draw in the three bases and home plate in the four corners of the diamond.

3. Now, using green paint, brush in some grass around your diamond.

4. Finally, with the black eyeliner pencil, draw in a stick-figure pitcher, who has thrown a tiny white ball from the pitcher's mound—your cheek!

One Step Further

What You'll Need:
baseball uniform • baseball • bat

If you're a true fan, grab a bat, ball, and uniform and look like a pro. Batter up!

Nifty Fact

Baseball began in the eastern part of the United States in the middle of the 1800s. Today, it is considered the most popular sport in America and is called our "national pastime."

28

A Vicious Vampire

Count Dracula would drool over this bloody-good face!

What You'll Need

- white, red, and black paints
- paintbrush
- black eyeliner pencil
- sponge
- red lipstick

Directions

1. A vampire has to have "deathly" white skin, so start by sponging white paint all over your face, including your eyebrows, and let it dry.

2. Then, with blood-red lipstick, outline your lips and fill them in completely.

3. How about using black eyeliner pencil or black paint to create new eyebrows over your whitened ones? Severely angled eyebrows will make you look super sinister!

4. Now, with eyeliner pencil, outline your eyes. Then extend your hairline into a "widow's peak" as shown.

5. Finally, use eyeliner pencil again to create teeth marks on your neck, and you'll be ready to party when the sun goes down. Read on for a fang-tastic tip!

One Step Further

What You'll Need
fake fangs (from a costume shop)

Every stylish vampire has fangs. You can buy fake fangs at a costume shop, or create some fangs yourself by painting them over your lower lip and down your chin as shown above. A tiny drop of blood created by your lipstick wouldn't "hurt" either.

Queen of Hearts

Although the Queen of Hearts from Alice in Wonderland was mean and nasty, you can make your queen a real sweetheart!

What You'll Need

- red and black paints
- paintbrush
- gold glitter

Directions

1. Give your queen a "sweetheart" look by drawing different-sized hearts on each cheek with red paint.

2. Before some of the hearts are completely dry, sprinkle some gold glitter inside a heart or two for a special romantic or royal look.

3. When the paint is dry, draw an arrow shooting through one of the hearts using black paint.

One Step Further

What You'll Need:
yellow construction paper • scissors • stapler • glue

Using construction paper, a stapler, and glitter, design a crownlike headband. Refer to the illustration above and to the Cheshire Cat on p. 16. Now your queen will have a truly regal touch!

Happy-Sad Face

You'll have to stop clowning around to paint this one on right. Don't worry, be happy!

What You'll Need

- red, white, black, and blue paints
- paintbrush
- sponge

Directions

1. First, sponge white paint all over your face and let it dry completely.

2. Next, paint a red mouth turned up in a smile on the right side of your face. On your left side, paint the mouth going down in a frown.

3. Now, outline your right eye in blue with the corner turned up. Your left eye will be outlined in blue also, but turn the corner down. You can use black paint to draw a teardrop on your left cheek to make that side really have the blues!

4. Add a few extra lines to emphasize your smile and frown. Grab a hanky to make the effect complete!

Lucky Ladybug

You'll be cute as a bug with this adorable face. But don't fly away before you gather your compliments.

What You'll Need

- orange and black paints
- paintbrush
- black eyeliner pencil
- sponge

Directions

1. Begin your ladybug by using your eyeliner pencil to draw a half circle on the bottom half of your face as shown. Then sponge in orange paint and let it dry.

2. Next, paint in black ladybug spots and a line down the middle of your half circle to indicate two wings.

3. Now paint in a black spot between your eyes for the ladybug's head. Add two antennae.

4. Finally, add six little legs and your ladybug is ready to fly, bringing everyone good luck!

What You'll Need:
pipe cleaners • headband

One Step Further

Try bending pipe cleaners around a plastic headband for more realistic antennae (see Madame Butterfly, page 14). You're sure to have better "reception" that way! And, since folklore tells us you can make a wish on a ladybug, why don't you close your eyes and try it!

Mary's Little Lamb

Paint on this face and your friends are sure to follow you wherever you may go!

What You'll Need

- white, pink, and black paints
- paintbrush
- sponge
- petroleum jelly
- cotton balls

Directions

1. Begin by using a sponge to rub white paint all over your face. Then let your woolly face dry.

2. Next, with black paint, draw eyelashes on your upper and lower lids to make big, innocent lamb eyes. Then paint yourself a cute pink nose. (If you don't have pink paint, create it by mixing red and white paint.)

3. Finally, pull apart some of the cotton balls. Then put petroleum jelly on your cheeks and stick on the cotton. Now your lamb is cute enough to give a snuggly hug!

One Step Further

What You'll Need:
pink ribbon • bell

Put a pink bow around your neck and you'll have Mary and Little Bo Peep wanting to take you home! You can even tie a bell to your ribbon and hang it around your neck so Little Bo Peep will always be able to find you.

Jigsaw Jackie

Don't let this face puzzle you. Just carefully follow each step and you'll see how your face will fall right into place!

What You'll Need

- any paints you choose, plus black
- paintbrush
- black eyeliner pencil

Directions

1. Paint the scene of your choice using whichever colors you like. It's best to keep the scene simple by drawing just one object, such as a house or a car.

2. Next, after your face has dried, use the black eyeliner pencil to draw in jigsaw lines as shown. Use the puzzle piece shown here as a guide.

3. Finally, black out several of the "pieces" you created when you drew in the jigsaw lines in the previous step. Then have your friends and family guess what part of your puzzle is missing.

Patch-Up Job

Your face will look as comfortable as a quilt with this snuggly face.

What You'll Need

- red, blue, white, green, and yellow paints
- paintbrush
- black eyeliner pencil

Directions

1. With black eyeliner, draw a grid pattern over your face as shown.

2. Now paint each box with different colors. Some boxes can be several colors, some can have designs in them, and some can even show objects such as flowers, hearts, or lightning bolts.

3. Go up to your mom or dad and wrap yourself around them for a warm hug!

Spacey Face

3

Friends are sure to revolve around you when they see this spacey face. It's out of this world!

- yellow, gray, blue, and brown paints
- paintbrush

- black eyeliner pencil
- gold glitter
- petroleum jelly

1. Using yellow paint, make a bright sun on your nose. Just as your nose is the center of your face, the yellow sun will be the center of the solar system you create.

2. Now it's time to add in the orbits of the nine planets in our solar system. Using the black eyeliner, paint in as many of these as you can. They will be represented by circles around your "sunny" nose.

3. Then, using different shades of gray, blue, and brown, paint in the planets themselves. Use the diagram to help you see the position of each planet, and remember to paint the rings on Saturn.

4. How about adding some stars by dabbing petroleum jelly on your face here and there, then sprinkling on some glitter? That will make this face a real dazzler!

Did you know that the term *solar system* comes from the word *sol*, which means "sun" in Latin? Our sun is a star, and its immense gravitational pull keeps the nine planets orbiting around it. It keeps asteroids, comets, and meteoroids orbiting it, too.

2

Radical Rainbow

It won't have to rain for you to show up wearing this colorful face.

What You'll Need

- red, orange, yellow, green, blue, black, violet (mix of red and blue), and indigo (mix of blue and violet) paints
- paintbrush
- gold glitter

Directions

1. Starting at the bottom left corner of your chin, paint an arc with violet paint. This will be the shortest arc, and it will end at the bottom right corner of your chin.

2. Once that arc is dried, paint an indigo arc on top of it. After your indigo arc is dry, paint a blue arc above it. Let dry.

3. Next, paint a green arc, then a yellow, an orange, and a red one. Remember, all colors must be touching one another, so leave enough drying time between painting different colors so they don't run together.

4. Finally, paint a little pot of gold on your neck just under the rainbow, using black and yellow paints. While the yellow paint is still damp, sprinkle glitter on it to make your gold really shine!

Nifty Fact

How can you remember the order of the colors in a rainbow? You can with a device called a mnemonic (nih-MON-ik). A mnemonic is simply a tool used to remember something. Now memorize this very odd name—Roy G. Biv—and you'll always remember the correct color order of a rainbow. The name is an abbreviation for **R**ed, **O**range, **Y**ellow, **G**reen, **B**lue, **I**ndigo, and **V**iolet.

Kissy Face

Your face will be extra lovable when you plant these paint kisses on your own cute face.

What You'll Need

- red paint
- paintbrush
- black eyeliner pencil

Directions

1. First, draw lips on your cheeks and forehead with black eyeliner. You can decide exactly how many kisses you want to "plant"—it's up to you!

2. Then fill in the lips with red paint and you're ready to blow kisses to your family and friends.

One Step Further

What You'll Need:
red construction paper • bobby pins

Cut lips out of red construction paper and bobby pin them to your hair. Now you can make Valentine's Day any time of the year.

Eyeball Head

You'll be quite an eyeful with this face. Here's looking at you, kid!

What You'll Need

- black, blue, and green paints
- paintbrush
- black eyeliner pencil
- petroleum jelly
- cotton balls

Directions

1. Begin this bug-eyed face by making eyeballs out of the cotton. Paint the colored part of each eye blue or green, then after it dries, put a black pupil in the center of each.

2. Next, dab spots of petroleum jelly on your cheeks, forehead, neck, and nose. Press your eyes firmly to the petroleum jelly and look out!

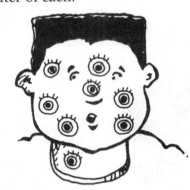

3. Finally, with black eyeliner, draw in eyelashes above each cotton eyeball.

One Step Further

What You'll Need:
pipe cleaners • construction paper • stapler

If you have any eyeballs left over, stick them on the ends of pipe cleaners and staple them to a construction-paper headband as shown. You remember how to make a headband, don't you? If not, refer to the Cheshire Cat on page 16. Now walk around and let your eyeballs bob, but be sure to watch where you're going!

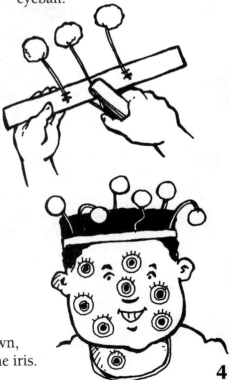

Nifty Fact

The colored part of the eye—be it brown, blue, gray, green, or hazel—is called the iris.

Pizza Face

Are you hungry? Try whipping up a quick pizza! You'll have your friends wanting to order take-out.

What You'll Need

- red, black, brown, and white paints
- paintbrush
- petroleum jelly
- cotton ball

Directions

1. In making a pizza face, first things first! Start with the crust by mixing brown and white paints until you get a creamy, crusty color. Then, paint this new color thickly around the edges of your face.

2. Now, slop on some sauce, using red paint to cover your face inside the crust.

3. Once the pizza is cooked (in other words, dry), "slice" your pizza with straight lines of black paint and add cheese with dabs of white paint.

One Step Further

Do you like your pizza with everything on it? Add mushrooms, green peppers, pepperoni, olives, and meatballs by mixing and matching paints. Mm, mm, good!

Candy Cane Kid

If you've got a sweet tooth, how about a sweet face to match? Be careful not to spoil your appetite by painting this delicious face too close to dinnertime!

What You'll Need

- red and white paints
- paintbrush
- black eyeliner pencil
- candy canes

Directions

1. With black eyeliner, draw the outline of as many candy canes as you can fit on your face. Use the candy cane to the left as a model.

2. Now carefully paint diagonal white stripes inside each candy cane, leaving space for red stripes in the next step. Let the paint dry completely.

3. Add red stripes in between the white ones and your candy canes will look good enough to gobble up.

4. Finally, hang some candy canes (still in their wrappers) on your ears. They'll be quite handy if you start craving a real candy snack.

Flower Child

You may smell like paint and not like a rose, but this face is definitely a good pick!

What You'll Need

- any color paints you choose, plus green
- paintbrush
- black eyeliner pencil

Directions

1. First, choose your two favorite flowers and draw black outlines of them on your cheeks, with the stems running down your neck. We have chosen a daisy and a tulip, but you can create the bouquet of your choice.

2. Now paint in your flowers with bright colors, and add green leaves on your stems. What a beautiful bouquet you've blossomed into!

3. How about a vase for your lovely facial flowers? Paint one on your neck and your flowers will have a place to dunk and grow.

One Step Further

What You'll Need:
real flowers

If you can find a real flower or two, put them in your hair. Then carry a bouquet and you'll really look like a flower child!

Scrumptious Salad

Toss this idea around and create a face that may look green but sure is healthy.

What You'll Need

- green, brown, red, yellow, orange, white, and black paints
- paintbrush

Directions

1. Paint a brown salad bowl on the bottom half of your face. The rim should reach to right under your nose, and the base should cover your chin. When you've finished filling it in, it will look like a big chocolate smile!

2. Next make various shades of green for different kinds of lettuce. Start with green paint, then add different amounts of white or black to it to create the different shades. Iceberg lettuce, for instance, would be green with a lot of white in it, whereas spinach leaves would be a darker green with black in it.

3. Now paint a bowlful of different lettuce leaves.

4. For fun, "toss in" some red tomatoes, orange carrots, white mushrooms, and red and yellow peppers. Be creative, but think healthy when choosing your ingredients.

What You'll Need:
a real fork and spoon • a two-foot piece of yarn

One Step Further

You can "serve" your salad more easily if you carry a salad spoon and fork around your neck. Simply tie a spoon and fork to a piece of yarn and make a utensil necklace!

35 Foot Face

There's nothing like the pitter-patter of little feet. When you're through painting this one, you'll want to give yourself a hand!

What You'll Need

- white and black paints
- paintbrush
- sponge

Directions

1. First, sponge white paint all over your face and let it dry.

2. Now, using the illustration as a guide, paint black footprints walking all over your face. You can start from one cheek and walk across your nose to the other cheek. Or, you can have your footprints "get lost" on your face and go every which way, even down your neck.

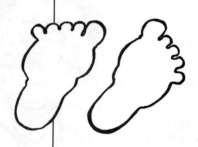

Rudolph, the Red-Nosed Reindeer

This doe-eyed dear of a deer makes a great Christmastime face. But you'd better not step outside—you may find yourself wanting to take flight!

What You'll Need

- brown and red paints
- paintbrush
- black eyeliner pencil
- petroleum jelly
- cotton ball
- sponge

Directions

1. First, dip a sponge in brown paint, pat the color all over your face, and let it dry.

2. Then, with black eyeliner, make innocent-looking deer eyes by painting in long eyelashes on big round eyes as shown.

3. Next, paint a cotton ball red and let it dry. Then stick this red nose on your own by using enough petroleum jelly to hold it in place. Now look for Santa and get ready to lead the way.

One Step Further

What You'll Need:
stiff brown cardboard • masking tape • paper headband • tape

Cut out cardboard antlers and use tape to secure them onto the back of a headband. (For how to make a headband, refer to the Cheshire Cat, page 16.) Then you're ready to lead your friends across the sky.

Father Time

Time will stand still when you set the hands of your clock face, but you can still run around and show your friends your timely creation.

What You'll Need

- white and black paints
- sponge

Directions

1. To create the clock face, dip your sponge into white paint and cover your entire face.

2. When your clock face is dry, paint on black numbers from 1 to 12 around the perimeter. Plan ahead before adding all the numbers so you'll be sure to have enough room for all twelve. For instance, you can start with 3, 6, 9, and 12, then fill in the other numbers, or you can put a tiny dot where each number will go so you can tell roughly how much space you'll have for each numeral.

3. Now pick your favorite time of day. Then draw the hour hand and the minute hand to show that time. Simple arrows make good clock hands, but you can make up different ways of pointing to the time, like pointing fingers on the ends of tiny hands.

One Step Further

What You'll Need:
paints of your choice for coloring in your decorated clock

You can decorate the face of your clock with flowers, hearts, whatever you want. You can also leave it plain white, but whatever you do, do it on your own time!

Miss Liberty

Be a symbol of the land of the free and the home of the brave and you'll have a lot of people saluting you.

What You'll Need

- green paint
- sponge
- silver and gold glitter
- plastic headband
- aluminum foil
- flashlight

Directions

1. First, if you have long hair, make sure to put it up in a bun to look even more like Miss Liberty. Then mix a small amount of glitter into some green paint for a shiny bronze look. Sponge the mixture onto your face and neck.

2. Miss Liberty wouldn't look right without her crown, so let's make one. Begin by rolling up pieces of aluminum foil into spikes that are pinched at one end into a point. Then attach these spikes to the base of the crown (a plastic headband) by curling the unpointed ends around the headband a few times and squeezing the foil into place. Make sure to look at our illustration for help on this one.

3. Wrap a small flashlight in aluminum foil and carry with arm raised high and proud!

Nifty Fact

The seven spikes on Miss Liberty's crown represent the light of liberty shining on the seven seas and the seven continents.

Picasso Face

Beauty is in the face of the beholder. This face may look weird, but it sure is artistic.

What You'll Need

- red, yellow, white, and green paints
- paintbrush
- black eyeliner pencil

Directions

1. First, use black eyeliner to draw a collection of eyes, lips, noses, and ears on different parts of your face. For instance, you can put a nose on your cheek, an ear on your forehead, and an eye on your chin. Anything goes with this face!

2. Now color in your face parts using bright primary colors. Let go and be artistic!

Patched Pirate

You'll have people ready to walk the plank when they see this scary face.

What You'll Need

- red and black paints
- paintbrush
- black eyeliner pencil
- charcoal

- black construction paper (optional)
- black yarn (optional)
- hole puncher (optional)

Directions

1. First, rub charcoal on your chin and cheeks to indicate a stubbly beard.

2. Then, with black paint, draw an eyepatch around one eye. If you prefer, you can cut an eyepatch from black construction paper, punch two holes in it, then string it around your head with black yarn.

3. Next, again using black paint, add a mustache with curly tips.

4. Finally, with red paint, draw a jagged scar on your cheek, and use black eyeliner to draw black stitch lines. You've had a lot of fights on the high seas!

One Step Further

What You'll Need:
aluminum • cardboard • red scarf • earring

Borrow a dangling clip-on earring (or a pierced one if you have pierced ears) and wear it on one ear as pirates do. You can also create a silvery saber by molding aluminum foil around a cut piece of cardboard. The illustration above will give you some ideas. Finally, tie a red scarf around your head and people will probably start saying, "Hi, matey!" when you walk by.

Nifty Fact

In their raucous adventures on the high seas, pirates also came to be known as buccaneers, picaroons, and sea rovers.

Frankie Stein

With this gruesome face, you can be Frankenstein's little brother or sister! You'll see the family resemblance in the neck and forehead.

What You'll Need

- green, red, and black paints
- paintbrush
- sponge
- masking tape

Directions

1. First, sponge green paint all over your face and let it dry.

2. Then, with black paint, draw stitches on your forehead, over your nose, and on your neck and cheek. Red drops of blood oozing from some of the stitches will look good and gory!

3. Now draw circles around your eyes with black paint for a hollow-eyed look.

4. Finally, "screw" your head to your neck with some homemade bolts made from two pieces of masking tape rolled with the sticky side out.

Nifty Fact

The title character of Mary Shelley's classic gothic novel *Frankenstein* is actually the doctor who creates the monster. In the book, Dr. Frankenstein never names the dead creature he restores to life.

Piano Player

This could be a noteworthy experience for you!

- black and white paints
- paintbrush
- black eyeliner pencil
- gold glitter

Directions

1. Using black eyeliner, sketch as many piano keys across the bottom of your face as you can. Do this by first drawing two horizontal lines from ear to ear, then connecting them with vertical lines from your nose to your chin as shown.

2. Next, fill in the keys with white paint and let dry.

3. Now draw black keys on alternating lines, as you see in the illustration.

4. Once your keyboard is complete, draw some musical notes with black eyeliner on your forehead, then fill them in with black paint.

5. While the notes are still damp, sprinkle on some gold glitter so your music will sparkle.

What You'll Need:
top hat and cane (optional)

One Step Further

Draw in one or two hands on the upper portion of your face. If available, grab a showman's top hat and cane and play, play, play!

Chief Running Brook

When it comes to creating the face of a Native American warrior, you can be the master of your own design!

What You'll Need

- red, blue, yellow, green, and orange paints

Directions

1. Starting with the blue paint, draw a diagonal line on each cheek. Use your fingers just like a real Indian applying war paint.

2. Now use your fingers again to paint red and green lines, too.

3. Next, draw a circle on each cheek with orange paint and fill it in with yellow paint, making two bright suns with orange and yellow rays.

4. You can draw whatever designs you want, choosing from any color you have on hand. War paint doesn't have to be warlike—it can be festive, too!

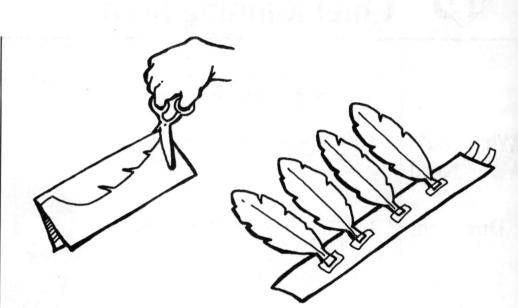

One Step Further

What You'll Need:
real or paper feathers • tape • colored construction paper • scissors

You can also make a headband to go with your Indian face. Start by referring to the headband in Cheshire Cat, page 16. Then cut feather shapes from colored construction paper or better yet, use real feathers if they're available. Now tape the feathers to your headband for a wild headdress!

Nifty Fact

Did you know that the first Native Americans came to America from Asia more than 20,000 years ago?

44

Laughing Leopard

You'll be so spotted after painting this face that some people might think you have the measles!

What You'll Need

- black and yellow paints
- paintbrush
- black eyeliner pencil
- sponge

Directions

1. Begin your great cat by rubbing yellow paint all over your face using a sponge.

2. Then, once your face is dry, paint black circles around your eyes. CAREFULLY fill in the circles with black paint.

3. Draw black spots on your forehead, cheeks, and chin. Make sure the spots are all different sizes because a leopard likes variety!

4. Now, with black eyeliner, draw leopardlike whiskers around your nose. Then smile and head for the jungle!

One Step Further

What You'll Need:
yellow construction paper • scissors • headband • yellow T-shirt

Make your leopard even more real by referring to the Cheshire Cat on page 16 to make a cat headband and ears. Then put on a yellow T-shirt or any solid-colored shirt. For even more fun, find an old solid-colored shirt and paint black spots on it.

Nifty Fact

Did you know that the leopard is the third largest member of the cat family? Only the lion and the tiger are larger.

I'm a Little Teapot

This face will surely be your cup of tea—and you don't have to be short and stout to enjoy it!

What You'll Need

- black and white paints
- paintbrush
- black eyeliner pencil
- sponge

Directions

1. First, using your black eyeliner pencil, draw a circle for the center of your teapot. Use the illustration to guide you so that you end up with your nose in the middle.

2. Now add the handle on one cheek, the spout on the other, a tiny knob in between your eyes, and a flat base on your chin. Once again, refer to the illustration for help.

3. Next, "call the kettle black" and paint it that way!

4. Finally, heat up your teapot so that it really gets steamed. Create a gray steam color by mixing a little black paint with some white, then sponge a puffy trail of steam coming from your spout across your forehead.

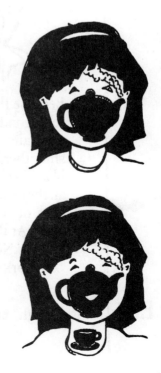

One Step Further

Are you thirsty? Why not draw a cup and saucer on your neck!

Anchor's Aweigh!

This face is a smooth sail. But if the waters get choppy, just drop anchor!

What You'll Need

- blue, brown, yellow, black, gray, and white paints
- paintbrush
- black eyeliner pencil

Directions

1. Using brown paint, begin your sailboat by painting in its wooden hull, which looks very much like the bowl you painted in Scrumptious Salad, page 45. Then paint in a brown mast as shown.

2. Once your hull and mast have dried, paint a triangular white sail connected to the mast.

3. Now paint half a yellow sun on your forehead, with a gray cloud starting to cover it.

4. What does your boat sail on? Water, of course! Using blue paint, set your boat afloat on a choppy, wavy sea.

5. Because the weather doesn't look good, maybe you should drop anchor and wait for smoother sailing. Using a black eyeliner pencil, draw an anchor line running from the back of your boat, down your neck. At the end, draw a tiny anchor. Now you can shout "Anchor's aweigh!"

Nifty Fact

To "weigh" anchor is to pull it up from out of the sea.

Home Sweet Home

You won't have to worry about losing your key when you paint this face!

What You'll Need

- red, white, and brown paints
- paintbrush
- black eyeliner pencil

Directions

1. Starting with a black eyeliner pencil, draw the frame of a house across your face. Your roof will be on your forehead, so you might want to pull your hair back.

2. Don't put that eyeliner pencil down yet! You'll need it to draw windows around each eye and a door around your mouth.

3. Finally, it's time to paint your house. How about white walls, brown shutters over the windows, and a bright red door? A brown roof would look good, too. And don't forget that chimney.

4. Why not welcome people into your home by drawing a mat on your neck? Have a friend help you write the letters W-E-L-C-O-M-E and then draw a box around the word. People will be sure to drop by!

Stopped-Up Face

Even if you don't have a license yet, it never hurts to stop a little traffic!

What You'll Need

- red, white, and brown paints
- paintbrush
- black eyeliner pencil

Directions

1. How many sides does an octagon have? If you guessed eight, you're right. Using a black eyeliner pencil, draw this eight-sided shape on your face as shown.

2. Have you ever seen a green stop sign? Of course not! That's why you're going to use red paint to paint your stop sign now.

3. Once your stop sign has dried, have a friend help you write the letters S-T-O-P boldly inside, using white paint. Then, as soon as you've added a brown pole down your neck, it's time to play traffic sign!

Corn Cobbler

You'll have to lend an "ear" to paint this corny face. But be careful, you might look so cute someone will want to take a nibble!

What You'll Need

- yellow, white, and green paints
- paintbrush
- black eyeliner pencil

Directions

1. First, with your black eyeliner pencil, draw the outline of the corn cob. Make sure your drawing lies across your mouth and stretches from ear to ear.

2. Still using your eyeliner pencil, draw in kernels as shown, then paint them in with yellow paint. To make your corn look even more realistic, paint some of the kernels a lighter yellow by mixing some yellow paint with a dab or two of white.

3. Complete your corn by wrapping it in green husks, which look a lot like leaves.

Nifty Fact

Did you know that Europeans first discovered corn when Christopher Columbus made his famous voyage to North America in 1492? He found the corn in Cuba and brought seeds back to Spain. Later, other explorers brought corn to different parts of the world so that by the late 1500s, corn had become an important crop in Africa, Asia, southern Europe, and the Middle East. It wasn't until the 1600s and 1700s that corn became a basic food item in the American Colonies.

Umbrella Head

You'll be singing in the rain but you won't get wet when you wear this face.

What You'll Need

- red and brown paints
- paintbrush
- black eyeliner pencil
- petroleum jelly
- silver glitter

Directions

1. Using the black eyeliner pencil, "open up" your umbrella by drawing a half circle on your face. The flat, bottom part should run across your nose, and the curved, top part should run across your forehead. Then add two lines, or ribbing, to show that your umbrella is indeed opened.

2. Next, with brown paint, draw a wooden handle down your nose to the bottom of your chin. At the end, make your handle go into a hook as shown.

3. Once your handle has dried, fill in your umbrella with red paint. When your umbrella has dried, get ready for a downpour!

4. Create your own rain with silver glitter. Dab spots of petroleum jelly above the umbrella, here and there on top of it, and down your cheeks. Then sprinkle on some raindrops!

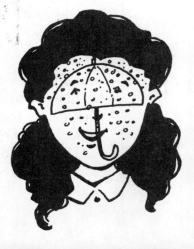